Who Does This Job?

by Barbara L. Luciano

PEARSON

Scott
Foresman

Editorial Offices: Glenview, Illinois • Parsippany, New Jersey • New York, New York
Sales Offices: Needham, Massachusetts • Duluth, Georgia • Glenview, Illinois
Coppell, Texas • Sacramento, California • Mesa, Arizona

We have many kinds of jobs.

I work in a bicycle store.

I keep you safe near your school.

I help people buy clothing.

I use a computer to do my job.

What job would you like to do when you grow up?

Glossary

clothing what people wear

job something that needs to be done

work what someone makes or does